Ulster Scots as She Tummels

A beginners guide to learning Ulster Scots

DOREEN McBRIDE

ADARE PRESS
White Gables
Ballymoney Hill
Banbridge BT32 4DR
Telephone/Fax: 028 4062 3782

© Doreen McBride, 2000

Published by Adare Press
Typeset by Mark McIlmail
Printed by Banbridge Chronicle Press Ltd.

ISBN 1 89949 613 O

ACKNOWLEDGEMENTS

*It is always pleasant to remember the kindly people who have
helped me.*

*First of all I owe an enormous debt of gratitude to my family,
especially my husband, without whom I would be completely lost
and to my niece Deborah.*

*Many thanks are also due to my old friend, Ernest Scott, was,
as always, a source of information and inspiration. I am also indebt-
ed to Philip Robinson, Irene McCullough, Lee Reynolds, Charles
Houston, Charlie Reynolds, John McIntyre, The Ulster-Scots
Language Society, The Ulster Scots Heritage Council and Dalriada.*

CONTENTS

INTRODUCTION

When I was a wee girl my Mummy used to take me to Skil-na-ban on the outskirts of Ballynure to visit her old aunts Bella and Lizzie.

At that time Skil-na-ban was an old farmhouse untouched by modern conveniences. It did not have electricity, gas or plumbing. Light, heat and delicious food came from an open fire with crickets singing on the hearth. Water came from an outside pump and there was a seven-seater dry toilet in the byre. In this strange, to me, environment my Mummy turned into a different person. I used to sit on a creepie stool beside the fire and gaze at her in wonderment.

To begin with, I could not understand a word! I could not understand what anyone was saying! They all sat around the fire speaking a different language, drinking endless cups of tea, eating delicious scones with home-made jam and laughing. Judging by the laughter the craic was mighty. Neighbours came, joined the fun for a while then disappeared. Mummy's aunts, Bella and Lizzie, bustled around, always busy, poking the fire, producing miracles of food, laughing, chatting, teasing and joking with their long black dresses sweeping the floor. An old man, called Andy, seemed to spend most of his life sitting on a stick-back chair next to the fire. He wore a duncher (cloth cap), smoked a pipe and was frequently asked to sing an 'Aul-Cum- all-ye.' I can still hear his harsh voice in my mind's eye. I could not understand a word but the others appeared to find it amusing. I was very puzzled.

One day, as we travelled home on the bus, I asked Mummy, 'What's an "Aul -Cum-all-ye"?' At first she could not understand what I was saying, then she laughed and translated. 'Doreen,' she replied, 'you had the pleasure of listening to an expert in the art of singing "an old come all ye."'

ye.""'

'What's that, and why's it funny?'

'Do you think it's funny peculiar or funny "Ha! Ha!?"'

'Both! It's funny peculiar because I don't understand a word of it and it's a peculiar type of song. And it must be funny "Ha! Ha" because everyone's laughing.'

'Right on both counts! You would find it funny peculiar because it's an old traditional type of singing. And it's funny "Ha! Ha!" because the singer describes local events and local people in a very humorous way. This type of song begins

"Come all ye fine people
And listen til me song.
It's only forty verses
And will not keep yez long."'

'Today Andy was singing about a dance held in an old church hall some time ago. In the past dances were held in big church hall. The downstairs room was used for dancing and the upstairs room was used as a ladies' cloakroom. People danced to the tune of the fiddle. During the night there was an interval and the ladies went upstairs to the cloakroom. In those days, there were no proper toilets so there was a line of chamber pots for the ladies.'

'Do you mean to say that women sat on chamber pots in front of everybody?'

'Yes dear. The only people present were other women and you must remember things were different in the past. Houses were overcrowded, bathrooms few and far between and people did not have the luxury of privacy.

Anyway, to continue with the subject of the song. One night some of the naughty fellows, who arranged the chamber pots upstairs before the dance began, put a little baking soda into each one. When the ladies used them, it bubbled up around their bottoms! This gave one of them such a fright she fainted and had to be carried home!

Andy's song was about that night. Everybody who was in the hall at the time was mentioned and it was very funny.'

'Why can't I understand what everyone was saying?'

'Because we were talking in the old language. The language of our forefathers. You don't hear it much nowadays and I think that is a shame.'

Lizzie, Bella, Andy and Mum are long gone. The house was tumbled to make way for modern dwellings. The only thing that remains is the remnants of the old tongue. What was it? How did it arise? Why has it persisted? The answers, like many answers, lie in the past.

The coast of Scotland is close to that of the North of Ireland. Ireland was once covered with dense forest so it was much easier for people living in County Antrim to trade with those in Scotland than with the rest of Ireland. This led to close ties between the two regions so that the Kingdom of Dalriada stretched across from the North of Ireland into Scotland. These close ties were strengthened in successive waves of plantations when people from Scotland were 'planted' in the Province of Ulster which encompasses the present day political entity of Northern Ireland and counties Donegal, Cavan and Monaghan. This influence is still felt today. The old language Ullans, (also called Ulster Scots) was the language spoken by people living in the lowlands of Scotland and parts of the North of Ireland. It is still spoken by 100,000 people today and is officially recognised as a minority language. A lot of its vocabulary has percolated into every day speech throughout Ireland.

Ireland is a small breeding population so, like it or not, we are all bred in and out of each other like rabbits. This explains why many present day nationalists, such as Gerry Adams, have Ulster Scots surnames. It is a shame, for such people to be denied part of their heritage. It is a proud heritage with its own literary tradition that influenced the great Scots poet Robbie Burns, who visited Ireland. Many famous people can claim Ulster Scots ancestry, including at least 14 American presidents and Davy Crockett.

The Ulster Scots language fascinates me. I love its flow, its powers of description and above all, the dry humour it can express. I do not pretend to speak it. I remember words and phrases and can, if I concentrate, read it.

The aim of this book is simply to share and deepen my own appreciation of a language that flows with apt description, wit and humour. I hope you enjoy it and will feel inspired to learn more from more academic studies. To this end a few helpful books are listed at the back in the appendix.

LUK GUID IN ULSTER SCOTS

Many people use phrases of a language when they wish to appear well educated. Personally I feel that a few in Ulster Scots is preferable to any other language. Ulster Scots has at least the advantage of being colourful!

The following list of useful phrases may be used for enjoyment or as an aid to making an impression. The choice is yours.

Phrase	Translation
Thon wud seekin a doag.	*That is utterly revolting.*
Ye couldnae het a coo on tha erse wae a bakeboard.	*You are a bad shot.*
Ye'r fond av yer belly.	*You like food.*
Ma ee's bigger nor ma belly.	*I put too much food on my plate.*
naw beg wae me	*do not like*
on tha broo	*claiming unemployment benefit*

cannae howl thur ain watter	*cannot keep a secret*
erse aboot face	*the wrong way round*
dannae fash yersel	*do not worry*
full as a po, or,	*drunk*
full as firty cyats, or,	
roarin full	
quit yer girnin	*stop* *complaining*
g'on or thet!	*catch yourself on*

Ah cud gut ye.	*I am very annoyed* *with you.*
a quare guzzling	*a long enthusiastic kiss*
whun hardy comes tae hardy	*when the real test comes*

Ye'd need ees in tha beck av yer heid	*You will find that is a difficult situation to monitor*
she cud ate hie aff a laft	*she is tall*
howl a wee while	*wait a minute*
Ah hae it in for hir.	*I intend to chastise her.*
Ye'r as green as ye'r cabbage lukin.	*You are very inexperienced.*
Ye luk lake something shot at an missed	*You look shocked*
Ah cannae put yin fit by t'other	*I am finding it difficult to walk*
Ye couldnae be lower if ye dug a hole an lay doon int.	*You carried out a despicable action*
wud ye luk at thon	*look at that*
niver while pooshy's a cyat	*will never happen*
thon's as sure as pooshy's a cyat	*that is as certain as pussy is a cat.*

BRAVE AN GUID WORDS TIL KEN

In any language there are many words with at least two meanings. I believe these are good words to learn. It is pleasant and seems economical of effort to be able to learn one word then use it in two, or more, ways.

Agane	again	Ye can pie me agane *(you can pay me when we meet again)*
agane	against	She's agane drink *(she's against drink)* Agane tha wun *(against the wind)*
aye	always	thon wean is aye greeting *(that child is always cying)*
aye	yes	Did ye see thon? Aye! *(Did you see that? Yes!)*
Ba	ball	he's fairly amused by a ba *(he likes to play with a ball)*
ba	cooperate	wud ye play ba? *(would you cooperate?)*
ba	baby	see thon wee ba *(look at the baby)*
Close	warm weather	It's close tha dey *(It's warm today)*
close	secretive	He's quare an close *(He's very secretive)*

craitur	animal	thon poor craiturs *(those poor animals)*
craitur	alcoholic drink	wud ye laike a wee drap av tha craitur *(would you like an alcoholic drink?)*
cut	style	wud ye luk at tha cut av hir *(look at her style)*
cut	drunk	he wuz half cut *(he was drunk)*
cut	embarrassed	Ah wuz cut *(I was embarrassed)*
Doncy	unwell	Ah'm feelin' doncy. *(I feel unwell)*
doncy	dishonest	Watch yer dink! Yon lad's doncy. *(Watch your money. That boy's dishonest)*
Fit	foot	Ye ha a quare beg fit *(You have a very big foot)*
fit	able	Ah'm fit for naethin'. *(I do not feel able to do anything)*
Lickin'	beating	He got half-tore an gie Sam a licking. *(He got drunk and gave Sam a beating)*
lickin'	currying favour	She's alwus lickin' roun' yer morr. *(She's always currying your mother's favour)*

lilty	energetic woman	she's a quare lilty
		(she's an energetic woman)
lilty	feeling full of energy	Ah'm lilty.
		(I feel full of energy)

N_{ear}	tightfisted	He's as near a body as ye iver met. *(He's as tightfisted a person as you are ever likely to meet)*
near	nearly	He darn near kilt me. *(He nearly killed me.)*
near	close	Ye wus near yersel! *(You were close to injury.)*

Ye wus near yersel!

Oany   only   There's oany tha yin wie o' daein it. *(There's only one way of doing it.)*

oany   any   Haes tha weather tuk up oany? *(Has the weather improved any?)*

Yer piggin'!

Piggin   type of wooden vessel which comes in different sizes, used as a ladle or to carry milk, etc.,   Gie me thon piggin *(Pass that piggin to me)*

piggin   very dirty   Yer piggin'! *(You are very dirty.)*

poor   pour   A wee pour av tay. *(pour a cup of tea)*

poor	power	He's lost tha poor av himsel'. *(He has become paralysed or weak.)*
poor	poor	Thon's a poor baste. *(That is a poor animal.)*
poor	pauper	Ah'm nae poor boady. *(I am not a pauper.)*
puke	to be sick	Ah puked up. *(I was sick)*
puke	unpleasant person	She's a raight puke. *(She's a very unpleasant person.)*

Raise	infuriate	Nick wud raise ye. *(Nick would annoy you.)*
raise	extend upwards	Thon hoose wuz raised in 1904. *(That house was extended upwards in 1904.)*
Tak	talk	It's a' tak. *(It's all talk.)*
tak	take	tak a turn *(take ill suddenly)*

tap	top	tap an tail *(top and tail)*
tap	smallest task	he niver does a tap *(he never does the smallest task)*
tither	confused or agitated state	Ah'm all av a tither *(I feel agitated)*
tiher	other	he towl me tither day *(he told me the other day)*

Ah'm all av a tither

Wak	walk	Ah cannae wak *(I cannot walk)*
wak	wake	Ah cannae gie til tha wake *(I cannot go to the wake)*
wak	weak	As wak as Holy watter en an Orange Lodge *(very weak)*
whud	move quickly	He's whuddin' alang tha road *(He's moving quickly along the road)*
whud	rumour	a whud gan round *(a rumour circulating)*

WATCH YERSEL!

Ulster Scots words may sound similar to English but have an entirely different meaning. This is very confusing! The words below are words to watch!

Ulster/Scots	English	Example of use
A	I	A feel wuntherfa *(I feel wonderful)*
ability	physical strength	A hae nae ability *(I have no strength)*
able	quick-witted	He's yin able wean *(he's a clever boy)* Yer man was able for him *The man in question was quick-witted enough to be able to cope with his adversary.* She's sure able wae tha tongue *(She is able to make a quick verbal response)*
awkward	perverse, difficult	he's yin awkward man *(he is perverse)*

an	and	A'm expected till work, an me kilt wae pains *(I'm expected to work and I am in bad pain)*
answer	suit	thon kep daesnae answer *(that cap does not suit)*
ark	wooden bin used for storing meal, oats, etc.,	See yon ark yonder? *(Do you see that wooden bin over there?)*

Batch, dirty, unpleasant type — thon batch leevin nixt ye *(that unpleasant person who lives next door to you)*

beak	shine fiercely	it wuz beakin doon *(it {the sun} shone fiercely)*
bite	something to eat	Wud ye laike a wee bite? *(do you require something to eat?)*
bliss	bless	may the Dear bliss ye *(may God bless you)*
bone	tackle, catch	A boned him the ither nicht *(I tackled him the other night)*
brave	quite, a reasonable amount	Cave Hill is a brave high hill *(Cave Hill is quite high)*
burn	small stream	thon burn's blin *(that stream disappears underground)*

Cabbage, stupid person — yer a raight cabbage *(you are a stupid person)*

cancel	spread gossip	she'll cancel it roun tha country *(she will gossip widely)*
chew	command to a dog to be silent	Chew! Jock, chew! *(Quiet! Jock, quiet!)*
choker	a polo necked sweater	A hae a choker *(I have a polo necked sweater)*
coy	lure, coax	ye eeny be tryin tae coy thon wee doll inty courtin ye *(there is no point in trying to coax that well dressed young woman to go out with you)*
crap	crop	put tha crap in *(sow the seeds, tubers, etc.,)*
Dress	scold, reprimand	A gae her a guid dressin *(I scolded her)*
drug	fine persistent rain	it's a raight drug *(it's a very wet day)*
Fail	lose weight	A hav failed awa tae naethin
fashion	habit	he's in the fashion av girning *(He has the habit of complaining)*
fierce	extreme	it's fierce cowl *(it's very cold)*
fill	make drunk	he haes filled hissel *(he has made himself drunk)*

Game	lame, crippled, sore	A hae a game leg *(I have a sore leg)*
gran	suit excellently	it'll dae gran *(It'll suit excellently)*
grew	greyhound	thon grew's a brave dawg *(that greyhound is a good dog)*
grip	a den of iniquity	thon's a raight grip *(that place is a den of iniquity)*
Ha	hawthorn	see yon ha *(Look at that hawthorn)*
hant	haunt	aul hants *(old familiar places)*
heap	a lot	a heap av dink *(a lot of money)*
hilt	pelt, hide	see thon hilt *(look at that hide)* neither hilt not hair av him *(no sign of him)*
hoke	dig	hoking spuds *(digging potatoes)*
hut	hit	A wuz hit wae a stane *(I was hit by a stone)*
Job	defaecate	A'm awa til dae a job *(I'm away to the toilet)*
Kitchen	meat, fish or anything eaten	A dinnae hae kitchen *(I have nothing to eat with potatoes)*

Lab	a lump	he has a quare lab *(he has a lot of money)*
labour	till, cultivate	A quit labourin an put it tae grass *(I stopped cultivating the land and sowed grass)*
lace	strike a heavy blow, beat	A'll give ye a quare lacin *(I'll beat you)*
lash	rain heavily	it's lashin' *(its raining heavily)*
lip	impertinance	he gae me a lat av lip *(he spoke to me in an impertinant fashion)*

Meat	food	A laike ma meat *(I like my food)*
men	improve in health, mend	A'm on tha mend *(I'm getting better)*

merchant	person of dubious character	he's a raight merchant *(he's a person of dubious character)*
mug	fool	A'm nae mug *(I am not a fool)*
Neck	cheek, presumption	he hes a raight neck *(he is very presumptive)*
Orders	requirements	she hes a'hir orders *(she has everything she could possibly want)*
Pad	path	an aul pad *(a familiar path)*
parcel	bundle of trouble	thon cyar's a raight parcel *(that car's a bundle of trouble)*
pass	do enough to avoid notice	a took a mouthfa tae pass maesel *(I ate a little to avoid giving offence)*
poem	gossip	he'll poem it roon the whole country *(he will tell everyone)*
Rail	very	rail guid *(very good)*
rare	unforgetable	I hed a richt rare time *(I had an unforgetable experience)*
rex	reach out	rex oot an help yerself *(reach out and help yourself)*

Scar	scare	it give hir a scar *(it scared her)*
seek	sick	A wus as seek as a doag *(I was very sick)*

It give hir a scar!

soda	a type of bread	Gie us a slice of thon soda breed *(pass me a slice of soda bread)*
steam	fun	he's great steam *(he's good fun)*
Wake	weak	Ah'm turrible wake (I feel very weak)
went	gone	A wud a went *(I would have gone)*
Yarn	story	yon's the quare yarn *(that's a good story)*

QUARE GUID WORDS

It is possible to bluff in a language up to a certain point. Think of all Irish posers, who give the impression that Gaelic is their mother tongue, yet they have only a few phrases of the language. It is equally possible to be an Ulster/Scot poser, but the trouble with posing is that the truth will eventually out. Increased knowledge is the best way to prevent this happening and it becomes necessary to learn some vocabulary. Personally I love these words. They are the words of my lost youth!

The following words are brave an guid words til ken.

Abane	Above
aff	off
agen	against
ain	own
airt	place
aisy	easy
amang	among
ax	ask

Bake	mouth
balderdash	nonsense
banes	bones
banter	light-hearted verbal teasing
bap	small loaf of bread

barge	scold
baste	animal
bates	beats, is better than
berk	annoying person
beetle	kitchen utensil used for mashing potatoes, or the act of mashing potatoes
birl	whirl round and round
blab	tell secrets, talk too much
blabbermouth	someone who talks too much

yer a raight blabbermouth

blarney	charming talk
blether	talk a lot of nonsense
blight	curse, disease
bloke	male
blootered	drunk
boke	vomit
brat	badly behaved child
bravely	feeling good
bungle	do a bad job

Canoodlin,	kissing and cuddling
carnaptious	bad tempered

champ	mashed potatoes mixed with spring onions or nettles or cabbage
chancer	someone who has the ability to make the most of opportunities
chitter	light hearted chat

Coo

clart	untidy girl
clatter	large number
cleek	hook
cleg	horsefly
clipe	tell tales
clipe-clash	someone who tells tales
clock	black beetle
clod	throw
clout	hit
coddin'	joking
cog	copy
colleen	Irish girl
colloge	intimate chat
contrary	obstinate
coo	cow

cooter	big nose
clootie	left-handed, clumsy
crabbit	cross
crack (craic)	good conversation, fun
creepy	small wooden stool
crig	hit
cub	small child
cyat	cat

D

Dab	good at doing something e.g. a dab hand
dae	do
daft	not wise
dander	walk
daub	smear
dearth	scarce
deave	deafen
dhrap	drop
din	noise
dinge	dent
dinger	something which goes well, going well
dirth	scarce
dishabels	old clothes
dote	pet, much loved person, usually a child
dotter	stagger
duds	clothes
duffer	stupid person
dun	exhausted, tired out
duncher	flat cap with a protruding brim to keep rain out of the eyes

dunnerheid	stupid person
dunt	hit, thump, nudge or push
dure	door

Ecker	school homework
eejit	silly person

Ah'm an eejit

ee	eye
een	eyes
efter	after
eeriwig	earwig
erns	errands

Fadge	potato bread
fags	cigarettes
falorey	harmless
farl	circular, flat griddle bread
fash	annoy
feckless	person who has no sense
feuter	fiddle with

fissle	small rustling noise
flaffin'	flapping
fleeced	stripped
flit	change house
flure	floor
fluster	confuse
fogey	old fashioned person
forby	as well as
foundered	cold
frae	from
freens	friends
frizzled	burnt
funk	fear
fut	foot
futless	walk awkwardly
Gab	chat, talk
gabble	rapid chat
gabbermouth	someone who talks too much
gad about	continually going out
galoot	silly person
gaunch	silly person
gander	go and look
gawk	stare
geg	joke

geek	odd looking man
gettin'	being attended
gie	give
girn	complain
glar	mud
gleek	look
glory hole	cupboard below the stairs
glower	stare crossly
glug	gurgle
goosegabs	gooseberries
gorb	greedy person
gomeril	silly person
gormless	person with no sense
gospel-greedy	goes to church frequently
gowl	shout
griskin	lean pork from pig's back
graip	digging fork
greet	cry
gub	mouth
guffaw	loud laugh
gumption	common sense
guid	good
gunk	disappointment
gutties	canvas laced shoes with rubber soles
gutters	mud

H

Hae	have
Half-one	small alcoholic drink
half-tore	drunk
hallion	clumsy person
hame	home
han	hand

handy	useful, nearby
hap	wrap up warmly
hash	make a mess, do a poor job
haveril	slovenly woman
heid	head
heid-the-ball	person lacking common sense
het	hot
hersle	hurry
het	hot
hidin'	beating
hinch	top of pelvic bone
hir	her
hirple	limp
hives	large itchy spots on the skin
hob-nobbing	associating with people of a superior socio-economic group
hoke	dig, search
hoof-it	go away
hooley	party
hovel	poor dwelling
howlt	awkward situation
huff	sulk
hum	unpleasant smell
hurl	throw
hunkers	sit on your heels
huzzy	cheeky young girl

I

Iggerant	ignorant
imperent	impudent
insense	explain
inundher	underneath
ins and outs	all that can be known
intil	into
itsel	itself
itchypoos	rosehips

J

Jaw	talk
jawbox	sink
jaist	just
jap	splatter, splash drops of a substance
jeg	prick, jab
jilted	to be rejected
jing-bang	a number of people
jitters	to feel nervous or shaken
joogins	pieces
jube	guess
juke	dodge, stoop down, avoid

K

Kale	greens such as cabbage or nettles
kaleyin'	out visiting and having fun
kantie	small
keek	peep
kelp	brown seaweed
ken	to know
kennel	kindle
Killinchy muffler	to hug someone by placing the arms around the neck

Killinchy waistcoat	to hug somebody by placing the arms around the waist
kilt	killed
kindlin'	fuel
kitchen	something, such as meat, to eat along with potatoes
kittling	kitten
knab	grab, steal
kyart	cart
kye	cows

L

La	law
lab	lump
labour	till, cultivate
lace	thrash, strike heavily
laid up	confined to bed because of illness
lally	lollipop
lammin	a beating
lashins	plenty
lang	long
larnin	learning
lass	girl
leer	sly look
lig	fool
lilt	a type of mouth music
lilties	foolish people
lip	impudent talk
loanin	lane
loof	open hand
lout	bad mannered person

| luk | look |
| lugs | ears |

Margiemore	mess
marley	marble
maun	must

Yer heids a marley!

measled	red and blotched skin
midden	manure heap
middlin'	not feeling 100 percent
mingin'	rotten smell
mitch	play truant
mizzlin'	light rain
moily	a type of cow which was born without horns
mollycoddle	be excessively protective
moose	mouse
mooth	mouth

morra	good morning
mortual	mortal
mountain dew	poiteen
muffler	scarf
munching	chewing
mutton dummies	see gutties

N

Nab	catch
nae	no
naebody	nobody
nancy	effeminate boy
naethin	nothing
nap	short sleep
nate	neat
neb	nose
nebby	inquisitive, nosey
nerd	stupid person
neuck	steal
ni	now
nicht	night
niff	smell
ninny	somebody without much spirit, easily scared
nitwit	foolish person
niver	never
nixt	next
noan	none
noo	now
Norn Iron	Northern Ireland
numskull	blockhead
nyammerin'	complaining
nyerps	upsetting thoughts
nyirm	nag or whine

nyitter	nag

O

o'	of
oagly	ugly
och	exclamation
och-a-nee	expression of sorrow or tiredness
oor	our
ousted	ejected
oot	out
oxters	armpits
oxter-cog	support someone under the armpits

P

Pachle	awkward person
pairt	a part
pairtner	partner
palaver	nonsense
paralatic	drunk
parritch	porridge
pech	pant, grunt
peerie	child's wooden spinning top
pernickety	fastidious, difficult to please
pester	annoy
piffle	nonsense
pinny	apron
pirty oaten	bread made with potatoes and oatmeal
pish	urinate, heavy rain
plooter	walk about in a clumsy fashion
po	chamber pot

praities	potatoes
pucker	flurry, state of over excitement
puff	breath

Quait	unassertive
quaff	drink a large amount
quakin boag	quagmire
quaking	afraid, trembling
quare	very good, or odd, quaint
quicks	young thorn plants used for hedging
quit	stop
quiver	shake

Raison	reason
ram-stam	move about in a clumsy fashion
rantin'	talking nonsense, usually in an excited fashion
rarin' to	eager to start

Ah'm rightly on!

redd up	tidy
reek	smell, smoke
rhodydandrum	rhododendron
rightly	had too much to drink, in good health
rigmarole	balderdash, or a long story
rip	rascal
riz	arose
roasties	roast potatoes
rubbitch	rubbish
rue	change one's mind, regret
ruinate	destroy
ruination	destruction
rummle	rumble
runt	weakling
rusted	refused

S

Sae	so
sally	willow
scally wag	rascal
scatty	demented
scoot	go rapidly
scrab	scratch
scraich	screech
screwmouse	shrew
scrimpit	minimum amount
scrounger	miser
scunner	sicken
sent for	about to die
sheugh	water-filled ditch
shuck	surprised, shook
simmet	vest
skedaddle	scamper off
skelf	a splinter

skelly	look at furtively
skelp	smack or slap
skimpit	tight fitting
skitter	diarrhoea
slabber	talk rubbish
skive	go away without giving a helping hand
sleeket	sly
sleg	abuse verbally, taunt
slider	slice of ice-cream held between two wafers
smittle	highly infectious
smush	rubbish
snib	lock, fasten
soda	type of bread made with baking soda
sonsie	full of life
sowl	soul
spae wife	female fortune teller
spew	to vomit
splatter	splash
splooter	splutter
sprachle	sprawl
spricklyback	stickleback
spulpin	mischievous boy
squeezebox	accordion
stane	stone
swarry	social evening with music and refreshments
stap	stop
stirabout	porridge
stocious	drunk
stoor	dust
strunt	huff, sulk

swally	swallow
swither	to be undecided

T

Tae	to
tanner	sixpence in 'old' money before decimalisation
tare	drinking bout
targe	bad tempered scolding woman
tattie	potato
tattie breed	potato bread
tatty	untidy, entangled
tats	tangled pieces of hair
tay	tea
thaveless	incompetent
thole	bear
thraple	throat
thrawn	stubborn
through-other	untidy
throw-aff	vomit
tiff	quarrel
tig	chasing game children play
til	to
titchy	very small
titter a wit	some sense
tonguing	scolding
toon	town
trigged out	dressed in best clothes
tuk	took
tuk bad	become ill

U

Umberelle	umberella

unaisy	uncomfortable
unner	underneath
unnerstan	understand
uppity	conceited, snobbish

V

Vent	freedom of expression or behaviour
veshels	dishes
vex	grieve, sad

W

Wa	wall
wadge	a large amount of
waff	a brief glimpse of
wally	silly person
wallop	to beat or flog
wean	child
weavers	spiders
weeda	widow
wee folk	fairies
weel	well
weemin'	women
weezened	dried up
whaling	beating
whammle	fling to the ground, throw over
wheeker	exceptionally good
wheen	a lot of
wheest	quiet
whelp	cub, pup
whinge	cry, whine
widna	would not
wile	very
wrought	employed by

wud	would
wunner	wonder
wut	wit
wuz	was

Yahoo	badly behaved person
yammerin'	grumbling
ye	you
yella	yellow
yella man	a type of honeycomb toffee still sold at the Auld Lammas Fair in Ballycastle
yer	your
yin	one
yince	once
yis	yes
yit	yet
yo	female sheep
youse	plural of you
yuck	something revolting

Yo

AUL COLLOGUE

A whole world of meaning may be expressed using one of the following phrases. Enjoy.

Thon's the wie o'it, and scurse a' ye can dae aboot it.
That's the way it is and there's nothing you can do about ot.

There's a slippy stane outside iverybody's dur.
All families will experience difficulties.

Between haein' an wantin' ye'll git by.
Be thankful for what you have and realise it is possible to manage without all your desires being fulfilled.

A ha year's a bra year.
Hawthorn's produce a lot of fruit during years which result in a good harvest.

It taks a steady han tae howl a full cup.
A large amount of money needs a wise head to handle it.

Tha bates Banagher an Banagher bates tha divil.
That is astonishing.

It's a quare aul world.
Strange things happen.

A wee pour av tay'll nay choke ye.
You must have a cup of tea.

APPENDIX:
ORGANISATIONS AND BOOKS HELPFUL IN ACQUIRING FURTHER KNOWLEDGE ABOUT ULSTER SCOTS

ORGANISATIONS

Ulster-Scots Language Society. This Society has been formed to encourage an interest in traditional Ulster-Scots literature and to promote writing in modern Ulster-Scots. The Society publishes a magazine, 'ULLANS'. Information may be obtained from the Secretary, c/o The Ulster-Scots Heritage Council 218 York Street, Belfast BT 15 1GY. Tel. no. 028 90 746939

Ulster-Scots Heritage Council. This organisation promotes the study of Ulster-Scots culture, history and language. Information may be obtained from The Secretary, 218 York Street, Belfast BT15 1GY Tel. no. 028 90 746939

Dalriada. Dalriada is the journal of Dalriada Celtic Heritage Trust which is recognised as a Scottish Charity. Information on cultural heritage may be obtained from Dalriada, Taigh Arainn, Glenartney Hotel, Brokick, Isle of Arran, Scotland KA27 8BX. Tel: 01770 302532. http://www.dalriada.co.uk.

BOOKS

ULSTER-SCOTS: A GRAMMAR OF THE TRADITIONAL AND WRITTEN LANGUAGE, Philip Robinson, published 1997, Ulster Scots Heritage Council, 218 York Street, Belfast BT15 1GY. This is an extremely useful informative work.

THE HAMELY TONGUE, James Fenton, published 1995, Ulster-Scots Academic Press, 17 Main Street, Conlig, Newtownards, BT23 3PT. This is a useful comprehensive dictionary.

SOME HANDLIN' The dialect heritage of North Ulster. Pupils and Friends of Ballyrashane Primary School, published 1990 North-West Books. This is a delightful dictionary written and illustrated by pupils of a school in North Antrim.

BARNISH, CO. ANTRIM DICTIONARY, M & F Montgomery, published privately 1993. This is a very useful local dictionary.

THE COUNTRY RHYMES OF JAMES ORR, the Bard of Ballycarry, 1770-1816, published 1992, Pretani Press, 78 Abbey Street, Bangor Co. Down

THE COUNTY RHYMES OF HUGH PORTER, the Bard of Moneyslane c. 1780, published 1992, Pretani Press, 78 Abbey Street, Bangor BT20 4JB

THE COUNTRY RHYMES OF SAMUEL THOMSON, the Bard of Carngranny, 1766-1816, published 1992, Pretani Press, 78 Abbey Street, Bangor BT20 4JB.

ACROSS THE FIELDS OF YESTERDAY, Hugh Robinson, published 1999, Ullans Press, c/o Ulster-Scots Heritage Society, 218 York Street, Belfast BT15 1GY. This book is written in Ulster Scots and is a delightful account of a childhood spent in the Ards, County Down.

WAKE THE PRIDE O DAN, Philip Robinson, published 1998, Ulster Scots Heritage Council, 218 York Street, Belfast BT18 1GY. This is a novel describing the effects of an Ulster Scots environment on a family.

ESTHER QUAEN O THA ULIDIAN PECHTS Philip Robinson published 1997, Ullans Press, 218 York Street, Belfast BT15 1GY. Philip Robinson retells and adapts a traditional Ulster Scots story. This work has beautiful black and white illustrations by Gary Hamilton.

FERGUS AND THA STANE O DESTINIE, Philip Robinson, 1999 Ullans Press, 218 York Street, Belfast BT15 1GY An adaptation by Philip Robinson of a tradition Ulster Scots story, beautifully illustrated in black and white by Gary Hamilton.

Other Books From Doreen McBride...

GREAT VERSE TO STAND UP AND TELL THEM
Edited by Doreen McBride

'Great Verse To Stand Up And Tell Them' captures the rich tapestry of life in Northern Ireland in comic verse. Every 'poem' has a situation story to tell and many are true to life. But that's only to be expected from a writing team including Maud Steele, Billy Ritchie, Seamus Lavery, Bill Nesbitt and Crawford Howard. Doreen McBride has edited this book. She has done an excellent job producing a book that provides an excellent read with verses suitable for reciting as 'party' pieces or performing at local festivals. **Price £4.99**

'A tool of rare quality for those wishing to perform a party piece or enter a local festival.' 'BELFAST TELEGRAPH'

A BIT OF CRAIC FROM BELFAST
by Doreen McBride

Illustrated by cartoon drawings and photographs of Belfast landmarks, this entertaining book takes us through the rich language usage of Belfast in a series of local anecdotes and stories, accompanied by a working vocabulary. The book is also enlivened by comic verse of local writers Crawford Howard, Raymond Calvert and Bill Nesbitt while Seamus Lavery's *'My Wee House'* adds a poignant reminder of the effects of inner city development. This book is a must for locals rejoicing in their heritage and for visitors who wish to capture Belfast's character. **Price £4.50**

'An entertaining book.' NEWS LETTER
'A gem of a book.' IRISH NEWS

HOW TIL SPAKE ULSTER
by Doreen McBride

In this hilarious beginners' guide to speaking the language spoken in Northern Ireland, Doreen McBride takes us by means of annotated cartoon and essential vocabulary to understanding some of the grammatical construction so essential to speaking the native tongue of her beloved Province. **Price £4.99**

'Doreen McBride did not come up the Lagan in a bubble.' Irish News

SPEAKIN' NORN IRON AS SHE SHUD BE SPOKE
by Doreen McBride

This local bestseller aims to help foreigners understand and appreciate the language spoken in Northern Ireland, which is affectionately referred to as 'Norn Iron' by local residents. As Doreen McBride explains, 'People coming from outside Norn Iron spake with a strange accent. It's very difficult to unnerstan them. After listenin' to people from all over, an' hardly understanin' wot thar tryin' til say, Ah've decided to do something about it an' produce a dictsunary til help foreigners spake proper.' This she has done and the result is hilarious. **Price £4.99**

'Essential reading' Gerry Kelly on 'Kelly' U.T.V.